The Perfect S
Mini Edition
North Amer

T0108851

Shot Placement for North American Big Game

by
CRAIG T. BODDINGTON

Artwork by
LAURIE O'KEEFE

Safari Press Inc.

An imprint of Globe Pequot, the trade division of
The Rowman & Littlefield Publishing Group, Inc.
4501 Forbes Boulevard, Suite 200
Lanham, Maryland 20706

Distributed by NATIONAL BOOK NETWORK

The Perfect Shot: Mini Edition for North America © 2005 Craig T. Boddington; artwork © 2005 Laurie O'Keefe. *All rights reserved.* No part of this book may be reproduced in any form or by any electronic or mechanical means, including information storage and retrieval systems, without written permission from the publisher, except by a reviewer who may quote passages in a reviews.

The trademark Safari Press ® is registered with the U.S. Patent and Trademark Office and in other countries.

ISBN 978-1-57157-320-9

Library of Congress Catalog Card Number: 2004091079

Printed in China

TABLE OF CONTENTS

DEDICATION

To my old friends, publisher Ludo Wurfbain and editor Jacque Neufeld, who have always had the really good ideas for books, and who, over the years, have made my work look so much better—and, most especially, to their son Rory, to whom the best wish I could offer is that he have as much fun hunting with his dad as I did with mine.

ACKNOWLEDGMENTS

The author would like to acknowledge that excerpts were taken from *American Hunting Rifles,* his previous North American book by Safari Press.

****

The publisher would like to thank the following photographers for the use of the photos seen throughout this book and on the dust jacket: Dusan S. Smetana, Gary Kramer, Len Rue Jr., Leonard Lee Rue III, Charles J. Alsheimer, George Barnett, John Ford, and Michael Francis.

INTRODUCTION

Since the publication of *The Perfect Shot: Mini Edition for Africa* by Kevin Robertson, dozens and dozens of people have suggested that a similar book should be produced when hunting North American big game. This book will be of value not only in depicting the game animals and optimum shot placements for them but also in describing the country, the hunting conditions, and the kind of shooting you might expect . . . and, thus, which rifles and cartridges are most suitable.

Mind you, there are no perfect answers. One of the exciting things about the great sport of hunting is that no two situations are exactly alike, and you never know exactly what any day afield might bring. But within the normal uncertainty that is part of the game, you can be—and should be—as well prepared as is humanly possible.

Luck is important in hunting, and while hunting luck often seems whimsical, I do believe the adage that luck occurs when preparation meets opportunity. To find opportunity, you will have to do your homework in researching a good area, and, once on the ground, you will probably have to hunt hard, and you should definitely hunt smart. I believe this book will help you improve your odds in the field on your North American hunts. So I wish you luck . . . and I hope this book will help you make some of that luck!

Craig Boddington
Camp Doha, Kuwait

This is a picture-perfect, side-on shot. Marked are the shoulder, heart, and lung shots.

MULE DEER
Tough to come by . . .
but not all that tough!

If you're talking about good trophy quality, I don't know of any North American trophy that is more difficult to come by right now than a really good mule-deer buck Mule deer live in country that is often some combination of high, rugged, and arid, so they have always been subject to more radical population swings than white-tailed deer. Hard winters and drought have always caused die-off, followed by a rapid rebuilding when conditions improve.

It is no longer true today. Much of the West is heavily developed—for recreation, for mining, and for the myriad vacation and retirement homes that dot the hillsides. Hunting pressure is a major factor today, and so are ski slopes, roads, logging operations, and mines that either preclude usage by mule deer or block access to critical winter range. Other facts are sagebrush eradication; livestock overgrazing; rapidly expanding herds of elk in some areas; and, where the two species collide, increased competition from whitetail. There aren't as many big bucks as there once were, and there aren't as many mule deer, period; in fact, I no longer know of any area where big bucks come easily—and there are lots of areas where the chances of finding a really big buck are virtually nil.

In terms of choosing the right rifle and load and making that perfect shot, what this means to mule-deer hunters is that you must choose wisely and shoot carefully. You'll work hard to get a shot, especially a shot at a really nice buck, and you cannot expect a whole lot of chances.

1

Mule deer are medium-size animals and, in most cases, a relatively quick-expanding bullet will be ideal for an instantaneous kill.

Shots at Mule Deer

Mule deer are often considered "long-range game," especially by those who haven't hunted them a lot. It is true that mule deer often live in country that is big, open, and extremely rugged and broken. There are times when a cross-canyon shot is all there is, and there will be times when open ground or an unfavorable wind precludes a close approach. Shooting at extreme distances is beyond the capability of most of us, and if there is even the slightest wind, I wouldn't attempt it. Note that, in the West, windy days outnumber calm days by a considerable factor.

I took my best-ever mule deer in Sonora, Mexico. We had followed a big set of tracks for a couple of miles, and I could tell by the way the spoor was winding and turning that the deer was looking for a place to bed. My guide, Beto Diaz, suddenly pointed ahead. A huge set of antlers protruded from low brush sixty yards away. The head was fortunately facing straight away, and just under that head was a very small expanse of neck. We shifted to find a slightly better angle, but the rest of the deer was hidden by brush. Since it was nearing midday, when breezes become unstable and swirl that small rectangle of stationary neck looked a lot better than my mental picture of the buck exploding out of its bed. So I wrapped into a tight sling with my .280 Remington, found the steadiest position I could, and shot the buck squarely in the center of that exposed patch of neck.

Most mule-deer hunts take place on ground that is broken enough to make close shots possible, or where there is enough vegetation, even if it is scattered. In most areas you might

The Perfect Shot: Mini Edition for North America

see deer at extreme distances, so very long shots are also possible. But most shots at mule deer come somewhere between the extremes. Over the course of thirty years of hunting mule deer under most conditions and in most habitat types, I believe most of my shots have come in the middle ground between 150 and 300 yards.

The latter distance may seem very far for hunters accustomed to taking whitetail from tree stands in thick cover, and, for the millions of hunters obligated to hunt their whitetail with shotguns or muzzleloaders, even 150 yards may seem a far piece! In real terms I consider 150 yards a fairly close shot. A shot at 300 yards is no longer close; it requires practice, skill, confidence, and a steady position—but the distance is not so great that it requires special equipment or a serious long-range rifle. Remember that a big buck may come out of a draw right at your feet. If you can handle any reasonable shot from point-blank to 300 yards, then you are well prepared for almost any shot at a mule deer.

Taking the Shot

I have never believed that mule deer were particularly tough. Although the average mule-deer buck is probably a bit larger than the average white-tailed buck, the largest mule deer and the largest whitetail are probably about the same. However, I do not believe the mule deer is as tough or tenacious of life as the whitetail.

In the spectrum of big game, none of our North American deer is particularly large or particularly hard to kill. However, a mule deer lives its life roaming big, rough country. It

In a shot like this, one needs to be careful to not shoot too much forward or backward.

When the deer is in this position, the shoulder blade covers a good deal of the lungs. The heart and lung/ shoulder shots are indicated.

The Perfect Shot: Mini Edition for North America

withstands brutal winters and hot summers, and in many areas migrates vast distances from summer to winter range. Hit poorly, or with an inadequate cartridge or bullet, a mule deer can travel vast distances and can be lost.

Much as I hate to admit it, the only deer I have ever lost was a mule deer. I missed the mule deer completely as it lurched toward the creek bottom. I was shooting a very accurate 7mm Remington Magnum with a good 160-grain bullet, so the issue was not an inadequate cartridge or a poorly constructed bullet. It isn't an excuse but a statement of fact when I tell you that I learned, too late, that this rifle shoots to a different point of impact with a bipod than it does without one. This is not uncommon. I knew this, so it was altogether my fault, and it was avoidable. I should have either checked the rifle with the bipod, or I shouldn't have given in to that last-minute thought that, given the open country, the bipod was a good idea. The only way to avoid potential disaster is to place the shot correctly the first time!

As with all game animals, the various sensible options include brain, spine, shoulder/ heart, and lung shots. For me the brain shot is out; except at very close range the target is too small to be certain, and even if you have the accuracy and the confidence, the trophy will likely be ruined. At normal shooting ranges for mule deer, the side-on neck shot is almost as risky. The target is very small; a high shot will only stun the deer, and a low shot will cause a terrible but not immediately fatal wound. Still, the central neck shot is deadly, and at closer ranges—with an accurate rifle and a steady shooting position—you should not rule out this shot.

Mule Deer

A frontal shot is also not my preference. On a frontal shot, if you aim where the neck joins the chest, you have a huge margin for a ranging error: Too high and you're somewhere in the middle of the neck; too low and you're in the center of the chest. However, your margin for a windage error is very small. Just a bit right or left, and if you're slightly high, you will miss the spine. If you're low, you will catch just one lung, or, far worse, your bullet will skitter along inside of the shoulder and do relatively little damage. On a frontal presentation it's far better to wait until the animal turns, the obvious exception being a very close and steady shot.

While I fully accept that a well-placed shot from the rear can be deadly, especially on deer-size game taken with relatively tough bullets designed for penetration, the risks are quite high. They go up exponentially as the bucks get larger and the cartridges get smaller (or the bullets get lighter in weight and more rapid in expansion). I won't tell you that I wouldn't take a "Texas heart shot" with an adequate cartridge and a tough bullet—if that was my only chance at the buck of a lifetime—but I can tell you that I have never taken such a shot at an unwounded deer.

Given an adequate rifle and a well-constructed bullet, I don't mind quartering-away shots, but my preference will always be to look for a presentation that is as close to broadside as possible, and I usually strive for a central lung shot. The aiming point will vary, depending on exactly how the buck is standing, but this means I'm trying to place the bullet just behind the shoulder and just under the horizontal midpoint of the body. This

9

The Perfect Shot: Mini Edition for North America

shot is not deadlier than a shoulder/heart shot, but is not less deadly. If the animal has just exhaled, a central lung shot will actually take effect more quickly than a heart shot; if the animal has just inhaled, then a final run of something less than one hundred yards is normal. The advantage of this shot is that it offers the most room for error of any fatal shot. Also, for game I like to eat, which includes all deer, less edible meat is wasted with the central lung shot than with any other body shot.

The Right Buck

With Rocky Mountain mule deer, the traditional standard for excellence has long been a "30-inch buck," a mule deer with antlers reaching 30 inches in extreme spread. This is a carry-over from the good old days, when fully mature bucks were much more common than today—but it was, is, and always will be a silly standard. Boone and Crockett's *Records of North American Big Game*, the oldest record book with the highest standard, doesn't even use extreme spread; instead, inside spread is measured. This is only one of several criteria. Point length and beam length are actually far more important; the hallowed Boone and Crockett book is literally full of bucks that are not 30 inches, whether outside or inside.

So, although many mule-deer hunters tend to be "spread freaks," spread is really just one dimension. At full maturity, the normal mule deer—of any subspecies—has bifurcated antlers (main beams that divide, then divide again) with four primary points per side. Eye guards are not as universal, nor as large, as on whitetail, and very good bucks often lack eye guards altogether. Nontypical points are those that exceed the typical configuration of "four by four plus eye guards."

Bucks with spreads exceeding 30 inches—and with all the rest—do exist, but I'm not certain I have ever seen one. I know I have never shot a "30-inch buck"—but I have taken some very good mule deer by record-book standards. Although spread is the common yardstick of excellence, I think it's far more important to look at point and beam length, then look at the antler mass that denotes a fully mature buck, and the rest be damned. The elusive 30-inch buck is almost nonexistent today, but there are lots of beautiful bucks with heavy antlers and long points that have spreads in the class of 24 to 28 inches. Today this is a good mule deer. Such a buck is very possible in many areas where Rocky Mountain and desert mule deer are found—and if the point length, mass, and symmetry all add up, such a buck can be a record-class specimen.

The other subspecies of mule deer are considerably smaller. Columbia blacktail and California mule deer do sometimes develop four-by-four antlers. Many good bucks are only three-by-three or even big forkhorns at full maturity, and this becomes more pronounced with all the other subspecies. Regardless of where you hunt and which subspecies you are hunting—and especially regardless of record-book score—the important thing is to know what kind of deer the area is capable of producing. If you find a buck that is above average for the area you are hunting—and if the buck pleases you—then you have a great trophy.

With a deer in this position, it is best to shoot for the lungs.

Rifles and Cartridges for Mule Deer

As is the case with most popular game animals, a big difference can exist between the deer you take on the last day to put in the freezer and the buck you might encounter if fortune smiles. The sad reality is that, even with the Rocky Mountain subspecies that is largest in both antler and body, the average buck taken is a 2½-year-old deer weighing little more than 150 pounds. But you need to be prepared for any buck you might encounter, not the buck you are most likely to encounter. The maximum body weight is as much as 500 pounds, but a wise, battle-hardened old buck weighing 350 pounds is not exactly the same animal as a young buck weighing less than half as much.

The 6mms and .25s are extremely popular in many areas, especially as "beginner's cartridges" for youngsters and ladies—but I submit that these are cartridges for experts. They lack the energy for long-range use, and lack the bullet weight to ensure penetration on the largest bucks. If you insist, the faster .25s (.25-06 and .257 Weatherby) are pretty darned good, but given the potential range and the size of the game I think serious mule-deer cartridges start at 6.5mm (.264-inch) and go on up to .30-caliber. This does not imply that magnums are necessary. Some of us will always prefer .270s, some of us will prefer 7mms, and some of us are .30-caliber fans—but I cannot imagine a better trio of deer cartridges than the triumvirate based on the .30-06 case: .270 Winchester, .280 Remington, and the grandfather, the .30-06 Springfield. These three cartridges will all reach out as far as most of us have any business shooting at game, but many of us feel better if we have this

13

Notice how low the heart lies in the chest. Heart shot is indicated, but it is so much better to wait until the animal turns sideways.

The Perfect Shot: Mini Edition for North America

"magnum performance" at our fingertips. So I think the very best mule-deer cartridge in the whole world is the 7mm Remington Magnum. It really won't do much more than the time-tested trio just mentioned, but it shoots a wee bit flatter, and its larger case engenders all kinds of confidence.

Bullet Performance

Deer-size game does not require today's supertough, penetrating bullets like the Winchester Fail Safe, Barnes X-Bullet, and Swift A-Frame. When fired from an adequate cartridge, these bullets will exit from any angle, which is good. Bullets that expand more quickly, however, will expend more energy within the animal, will do more damage to vital organs, and will generally result in quicker kills. So for deer-size game, I tend to lean toward bullets that expand more quickly—fairly conventional softpoints like the Hornady Interlock, Sierra, and Speer, or polymer-tipped bullets like the Ballistic Silvertip, Hornady A-Max, and Nosler Ballistic Tip.

There is one big exception. It is so difficult today to get a really big mule deer that you must be ready for any reasonable shot. I want a bullet that will expand, yet I also want a bullet that will penetrate should I draw a bad-angle shot. Historically, the Nosler Partition is one of the best bullets that combines both expansion and penetration in a single design. The front core, ahead of the partition, expands rapidly; the back core, protected by the partition, penetrates almost like a solid. Even today there are very few bullets that offer this combination. One that does is the new Swift Scirocco, combining a bonded core and heavy jacket for weight retention with a polymer tip for expansion.

Special Circumstances

Most of the foregoing concerns Rocky Mountain mule deer, or at least the larger subspecies of mule deer. In central California the deer are a mixture of California mule deer and Columbia blacktail, and they are small. The country is also patchy and tight, and longer shots are unusual. There the .243 is by far the most popular deer cartridge, and it's plenty of gun for our 125-pound deer. I tend to think other low-recoiling cartridges like the .260 Remington, 6.5x55mm, 7mm-08, and 7x57mm are even better. The point is that if you hunt smaller deer like the Columbia blacktail, you don't need as big a gun.

One important exception is hunting desert mule deer in old Mexico. This is one of the very few opportunities for a really big buck, except that not everyone will get one or even get a shot. In four hunts I've taken two bucks, which is well ahead of the average. Even more unusual is that I've taken both bucks in their beds. It's more likely that you will jump the deer, and you'll have a quick, panicky shot at a fast-disappearing form. The deer are not large in the body, but the shooting can be exceptionally difficult, and you have little control over the shot you get. Under such circumstances you want a fairly powerful rifle—no less than .270—and a bullet that will surely penetrate.

Wait till the deer stops, or lead the point of aim slightly. The heart, shoulder, and lung shots are marked.

WHITE-TAILED DEER
Oh, so common . . .
and oh, so difficult!

The white-tailed deer is the most popular and most populous game animal in North America. The whitetail is, however, no matter how numerous it might be, no pushover. It is an exceptionally wary creature, blessed with sensitive ears, sharp eyes, and a keen nose. By nature it loves cover, but it's also a homebody who knows its home turf intimately and doesn't need much cover to vanish completely. It is crepuscular, meaning it is typically most active during the twilight periods of dawn and dusk. It is also completely at home in the darkness and, with just a bit of pressure, is never seen in the daylight.

In all of its subspecies, it's pretty much the same deer, developing antlers that have fighting tines rising from a main beam. Wherever it occurs, it leaves much the same sign—the tracks and droppings and rubs and scrapes we whitetail hunters argue about endlessly. But exactly how you hunt it varies considerably depending on where you hunt it.

Safari Club International's record book subdivides the whitetail into seven regional groupings: northwestern, northeastern, southeastern, Texas, Coues, Mexican, and central American. It draws lines along political boundaries, and almost every regional category encompasses multiple subspecies. Boone and Crockett and Pope and Young are more conservative. They each have just one category for all white-tailed deer. The one exception is a separate category for the small Coues whitetail of the mountains of the Southwest.

White-tailed Deer

19

White-tailed Deer

Whitetails vary tremendously in size, but any decently constructed bullet in .25 caliber on up will kill with proper shot placement.

Shots at Whitetail

Unlike many types of game, most whitetail are relatively habitual, so to some extent you can control the shot you get through your hunting technique, and you can choose exactly where you set up. Even in the more open West, savvy bow hunters achieve considerable success by stand hunting along movement corridors between bedding grounds and feeding covers. The possible exception to this is Coues whitetail; they are thinly distributed in huge country and are generally less habitual than other whitetail. To this day archers have taken relatively few Coues deer, and they are considered one of America's most difficult game to bow hunt.

In the East literally millions of American hunters are obligated by law to use shotguns or muzzleloaders. Fully rifled slug guns and some muzzleloaders have enough accuracy to cleanly take deer out to 200 yards, but for most of those hunters, the practical range limit is around 100 yards. With such range limitations, it doesn't make sense to set up over a feeding field. You can take a stand in heavy cover, where trails suggest deer are moving between feeding and bedding grounds. Or, in heavy or mixed cover, you can use calls or rattling antlers to lure deer to the gun. In many areas deer drives—whether with human or canine "drivers"—are the traditional technique, and buckshot-loaded shotguns are often the arm of choice. Whether by choice or by law, if you limit your range with a bow, shotgun, or muzzleloader (or, for that matter, a handgun), you simply need to choose ground and technique that are likely to yield a shot you can handle.

White-tailed Deer

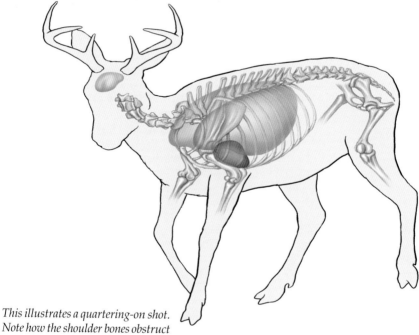

This illustrates a quartering-on shot. Note how the shoulder bones obstruct much of the heart/lung area.

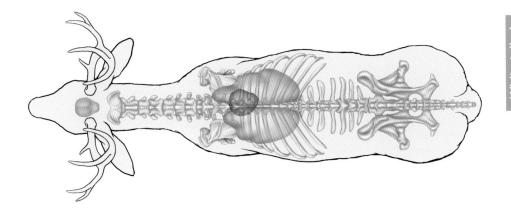

From this top view it really becomes obvious how small the heart and lungs are for a straight-on frontal shot. Also note, again from the top angle, how the heart is surrounded by the shoulder blades and the spine.

The Perfect Shot: Mini Edition for North America

Rifle-toting hunters have far more options, and indeed a shot at a white-tailed deer can take almost any form, from very close to very far. Close encounters are most likely to occur from a stand, or while rattling or calling, but they can occur almost anywhere. Longer shots are also possible almost anywhere. The deep South is famous for its huge soybean fields that draw deer like magnets. It's this kind of hunting that gave South Carolina gunmaker Kenny Jarrett the name for his famous "Beanfield Rifle"—slightly heavy, flat shooting, super-accurate, and designed to reach out across those southern beanfields. It could well have been a "cornfield rifle," because wherever grain is grown, white-tailed bucks are just as likely to be standing on the far side as on the near side. And one mustn't forget the power-line rights of way and logging roads that offer opportunities for longer shots even in the midst of heavy cover.

Very few whitetail habitats in the whole country are as thick as the famous brush country of south Texas. It's in this region that hunters developed the technique of calling rutting bucks by "horn rattling," simulating a fight between two bucks. If you're rattling antlers along the edges of thick brush, you may get a very close shot. But this country is crisscrossed by a grid of cut lines, the famous *senderos* of south Texas. It's always possible for a huge buck to walk under your stand—but you're much more likely to get a shot a couple of hundred yards up the *senderos*.

So it's almost impossible to categorize shots at whitetail. Several million whitetail are harvested annually, and it's probably fair to say that the average shot is well under one hundred yards. This is skewed by the fact that our greatest numbers of whitetail are found in the thick cover of the deep South, the Northeast, and the upper Midwest. It's also skewed by those millions of hunters who use short-range equipment. In the West shooting opportunities average a good deal longer, depending on how you hunt.

Really big whitetail are just plain hard to come by. Big, fully mature bucks aren't exactly uncommon in all areas, but a buck that has survived several hunting seasons becomes so elusive and, often, so nocturnal that it is almost impossible to kill. I would never advocate taking any shot that you aren't absolutely certain you can make. But there is no telling when or where a big buck might present itself, and your chances of bagging it are much improved if you can handle the full range of potential opportunities, from very close to very far.

Taking the Shot

White-tailed deer are amazing creatures. They have adapted to life in proximity with man, yet they have also adapted to the full range of harsh conditions, from the arid mountains of the Southwest to the bitter winters of northern Canada. Pound for pound, the whitetail is a fairly tough creature. Hit poorly, it is able to take a great deal of punishment, and it can cover a surprising amount of ground even if hit fairly well.

Of course, the whole purpose of this book is to avoid the difficulties—to make the "perfect shot" that precludes a lengthy follow-up. Unless the range is very close

Again it shows how hard a frontal shot is. This one is made even harder because the deer's hindquarters are lower than its front quarters. Heart shot is indicated.

The Perfect Shot: Mini Edition for North America

and you have absolute confidence in your ability to place the shot, I don't like the brain, neck, or spine shots. They are immediately fatal, or at least totally disabling, if executed correctly—but there is just too much margin for error. My preference is the central lung shot. From a broadside presentation, divide the body horizontally into thirds: top third, middle third, bottom third. For a perfect lung shot, follow the back line of the rear leg up and shoot into the bottom half of the middle third. From various angles away from the broadside, you must visualize where this area lies, but the good news is that, of all the surely fatal shots, the lung shot offers the greatest margin for error.

Whether the lung shot is immediately fatal depends a bit on luck. If the animal has just exhaled and is depleted of oxygen, a lung shot may well drop it in its tracks. If it has just inhaled, you may see very little initial reaction, but it should go down within sixty yards. The lung shot also offers the advantage of ruining less edible meat than the heart shot, but the heart shot is also a very good option.

The problem with a true heart shot is that it's a bit tricky, and you must consciously shoot a bit lower than most people wish to. From a broadside presentation, again divide the body horizontally into thirds. Follow the center line of the foreleg up to the center of the bottom third, and you have a heart shot. If you shoot high or you shoot a couple of inches too far back, you still have a fatal shot in the lungs. But you have very little margin for error if you shoot low or too far forward.

28

White-tailed Deer

In terms of effect, anticipate a frantic final run of possibly seventy-five yards with a heart shot. However, you can expect your deer to go down in its tracks if you use a fairly powerful rifle with a tough or heavy bullet and you break both shoulders while transiting the heart. Because of the very small margin for error, I don't like frontal shots; it's better to wait for the buck to turn unless, again, you are fairly close and very steady. The angle is dictated to some extent by the caliber you're using and the penetrating properties of your bullet. I don't like the so-called "Texas heart shot" on unwounded deer, but, especially if you're trophy hunting, I think it's wise to use enough gun and enough bullet that you can take any reasonable shot in terms of both range and presentation.

The Right Buck

Trophies are in the eye of the beholder, and this is perhaps truest with whitetail. Fully mature, big-racked bucks do occur throughout the whitetail's range. But in many areas a combination of short seasons and intensive hunting pressure render any whitetail taken in fair chase a truly great trophy. Some areas produce bigger bucks or have greater numbers of them than other areas. There are record-class bucks roaming the East and the South, but they are so unusual—and so difficult to hunt—that seeking one is almost like hunting a unicorn. In the regions that are harder hunted, most hunters are justifiably proud of any eight- or ten-point buck, meaning a total count of eye guards and fighting tines.

White-tailed Deer

At a slight angle, but this is not a hard shot.

The Perfect Shot: Mini Edition for North America

In other areas it's possible to be more selective. There are areas, like the Great Plains, western Canada, and some of the well-managed ranches of Texas, where buck-to-doe ratios are high and where a fairly large percentage of the buck herd lives long enough to reach full maturity. In such areas I have never thought in terms of record-book score. Instead, I think in terms of a buck that has reached full maturity: 5½ years old or, better still, 7½ and older. Such a buck may be a big 8-pointer or, more likely, a 10-pointer, or it may have more typical and some nontypical points. But it will have mass and character to its rack, and its body will be heavy and powerful. To me that's a trophy whitetail, regardless of how its rack scores.

Whitetail Guns and Loads

Choosing the right gun and load is complicated by the fact that whitetail vary tremendously in body size. The average white-tailed buck taken is probably a 1½- to 2½-year-old forkhorn buck that weighs less than 150 pounds. On the other hand, big northern and northwestern bucks can weigh over 350 pounds at maturity, and, throughout most of their range, bucks exceeding 250 pounds are occasionally encountered. If you wish to be armed for the biggest buck roaming your area, you need to keep this disparity in mind.

A well-placed shotgun slug will handle any whitetail that walks. The real secret is to consider your slug gun the same way you would consider a rifle for sheep or pronghorn hunting. Yes, the range is more restricted, but you still want all the accuracy you can get. Modern slug guns with fully rifled barrels do extend the potential range a bit. More important, they offer pinpoint accuracy—and even though the shotgun slug is a huge piece of metal, it's still important to put it in the right place.

So take advantage of rifle-barrel technology, and make sure you have top-quality rifle sights on your deer shotgun—preferably a good, light-gathering, low-power scope. Then spend time on the range discovering exactly what slugs your shotgun groups best with. If you do your homework, the handicap posed by a modern slug gun isn't all that great, and exactly the same applies to muzzleloaders.

If you hunt whitetail with rifles, the whole world is open to you. This doesn't mean you necessarily need a flat-shooting magnum. That depends on where and how you hunt. The .30-30 Winchester has probably accounted for more deer than any other cartridge, and it remains perfectly adequate for any deer that walks. If you hunt in close cover where shots much beyond one hundred yards are unlikely, then you aren't handicapped in the least with the good old lever-action carbine your grandfather carried—except that its traditional open "buckhorn" sights may be handicapping you. Good sights, either an aperture or a low-powered scope, won't extend the range of a .30-30 by much, but they will enable you to shoot faster and more accurately, especially under low-light conditions.

These days most rifle-toting hunters seem to have made the shift to scoped rifles in flatter-shooting, more versatile calibers, with the bolt-action by far the most popular. This is generally wise, because a flat-shooting rifle will work just fine up close as well as a long way out; a short-range brush gun cannot handle longer shots.

*From above. The lung area exposed to
the hunter now becomes smaller.*

White-tailed Deer

The Perfect Shot: Mini Edition for North America

White-tailed Deer

Caliber really depends a lot on where you hunt. In many states the .22 centerfires (.223 Remington, .22-250, et cetera) are legal. I have taken a lot of deer with these little cartridges, and they work, but shot placement must be extremely precise, and they do not have enough energy for longer shots. I don't think they're suitable for the largest-bodied deer, nor are they a good idea for trophy hunting anywhere; you're just too limited in the shots you can take. In Texas and much of the southeast, mild cartridges like the .243 and the .25s are extremely popular. They're just fine for the smaller-bodied deer in these regions and are excellent for "meat hunting" everywhere. But if you want to be prepared for the largest-bodied deer, and for any shot you might encounter, I think a step up is appropriate.

The good old 7x57mm is one of my favorite whitetail cartridges, which means that similar cartridges like the .260 Remington, 6.5x55mm, and 7mm-08 are also good. But for genuine all-round use under almost all conditions, old favorites like the .270 Winchester, .280 Remington, .30-06, and .308 Winchester are extremely hard to beat. I honestly believe that you do not have to have any magnum cartridge for any white-tailed deer hunting. But if a magnum gives you more confidence, then any of the magnums between, say, the new .270 Winchester Short Magnum to the .30-caliber magnums will certainly do the job on any whitetail, up close or far away.

I have often carried magnums on open-country whitetail hunts, and a couple of times I've been glad I had them. I took my best Texas buck way down a *sendero* with a pet 7mm Remington Magnum, and I took my best plains buck in western Kansas with a .300 Weatherby

Magnum. Honestly, in both cases a .270 Winchester would have done as well—but in both cases these were favorite rifles that gave me the confidence I needed to make a difficult shot. That "C" factor (for confidence) is always more important than the actual caliber.

Bullet Performance

White-tailed deer are tough, but even the biggest whitetail isn't all that big. Under most circumstances I like to use accurate bullets that will open up fairly quickly. Depending on the rifle, I use a lot of Hornady Interlocks, Sierra GameKings and Pro-hunters, and Nosler Ballistic Tips. I have also used a lot of factory ammo loaded with Federal Hi-Shoks, Remington Core-Lokts, and Winchester Power Points and Ballistic Silvertips. These are not "tough" bullets, but under most circumstances all are tough enough for white-tailed deer, and all will expand fairly rapidly and do a great job.

There are exceptions. If you're using relatively light calibers, especially for large deer, then you may want to consider tougher bullets like the Nosler Partition, Trophy Bonded Bear Claw, or Barnes X-Bullet to ensure you will get the penetration you must have. On serious trophy hunts for large-bodied deer, I often use fairly tough bullets like these. I want to absolutely ensure that I will have the penetration I need even if I have to take a bad-angle shot because, if the buck of a lifetime appears, I want to be able to take any shot with confidence.

White-tailed Deer

Watch those branches. Best to wait until the deer takes a step forward. Shoulder/heart and two lung shots indicated.

White-tailed
Deer

The Perfect Shot: Mini Edition for North America

Special Circumstances

The little Coues whitetail is the most obvious special circumstance. This is a very small-bodied deer; even a really big buck will rarely weigh more than 100 pounds. So, on the surface, a 6mm or .25-caliber would be a great choice—except that Coues deer live in big, rough country where shots on whitetail average a good deal longer. I have taken a couple of bucks at very long range, but most of my shots come at somewhere between 250 and 350 yards. That is still a far poke. Because of the distance, and because larger bullets resist wind better than small bullets, fast .270s and 7mms are good minimal choices. The really serious guys, like David Miller and outfitter Kirk Kelso, use .30-caliber magnums and apologize to no one for being overgunned.

Although I can't imagine the situation, reader mail over the years has suggested that, in some hard-hunted woods, the only way to avoid an argument about whose tag goes on a deer is to drop it in its tracks. Under these conditions a lot of hunters use cartridges like the .35 Whelen, .444 Marlin, and .45-70. Cartridges like these are not required for any whitetail, but if you want to drop your deer in its tracks, nothing will do it as dramatically as a big, slow-moving blunt-nose or roundnose bullet. Flat-point and roundnose bullets transfer energy more quickly, which is partly the reason the .30-30 is so much more effective than its paper ballistics indicate. So if you hunt in close cover and you're not worried about a long shot, borrow a page from the brush-busters and load up your .270, .30-06, or .308 with the roundnose loads most manufacturers still offer. You will see a difference in impact with any well-placed shot.

40

The heart and a good deal of the whitetail's lungs are well protected by shoulder bone in a shot like this one, and the margin of error either left or right is very small at this angle. This is not a shot to take offhand or from a wobbly position.

41

American Elk

Heart and lung shot indicated. Wait a second until the bull turns his head.

AMERICAN ELK
Our toughest deer . . .

Few animals on earth approach the majestic bearing of a mature bull elk. Great antlers thrown back, neck outstretched, it bugles its challenge in a high Alpine meadow—and it symbolizes the high, wild country of the American West. The most plentiful and widespread is the Rocky Mountain elk. The Rocky Mountain elk is a big elk with dark neck and legs and pale body, growing long-beamed antlers that, typically, will have six or, rarely, seven points at full maturity. Body size varies tremendously depending on genetics and food conditions, but a good average for a mature Rocky Mountain bull would be 700 pounds. Usually forgotten is the Manitoba elk, now restricted to isolated habitat in Manitoba and Saskatchewan. The Manitoba elk is somewhat larger than the Rocky Mountain elk, with similar antlers.

In the Pacific Northwest the elk are of the Roosevelt subspecies, a giant of an animal with bulls often approaching a half-ton. The Roosevelt elk is darker and blockier in build, and tends to have shorter, thicker antlers. In the valleys and foothills of central and southern California, the elk are tule elk, also called dwarf or valley elk. The tule elk is the smallest and palest subspecies, with mature bulls running around 550 pounds. Tule elk antlers are usually short-beamed, but seven, eight, and even nine points per side is common, the upper points often coming in a cluster or "crown" similar to that of red deer.

American Elk

43

Elk are notoriously tough animals and should ideally be shot when standing broadside, such as seen in the stance of this bull. However, before the shot is taken, wait for the animal to move its head straight forward.

Shots at Elk

These days most rifle seasons are held after the bugling is over, but there are some opportunities to hunt during bugling. If you're fortunate enough to hunt with a rifle when the elk are really bugling, then you can expect relatively close shots. The classic situation is for a bull to answer your challenge and come charging in, offering a shot at point-blank range. It usually doesn't work that way, especially with the best bulls. The bulls that come charging in tend to be the younger, satellite bulls, which you don't want if you're looking for the best bull you can find. The old boys are experienced and often have cows; they may answer you, but they aren't likely to run over you.

Even during the bugling season, and especially when it's over, terrain and vegetation will dictate the kind of shot you're most likely to get. In the Pacific Northwest the cover is incredibly thick, and almost all shots are at extremely close range. In high Alpine country, and in the big sagebrush meadows where elk love to feed, there are opportunities for fairly long shooting, but in the timber and oakbrush hillsides on the lower slopes things close in. With few exceptions, shooting can vary from quite close to quite far, with the average somewhere in the middle. I have taken a number of elk at less than 50 yards and a few from 350 to 400 yards, but most have been between 100 and 200 yards.

If undisturbed, elk are also relatively habitual unless there is a change in something like weather or food supplies. For instance, if you see elk feeding in a distant meadow at daybreak, but they fade into the timber before you can get to them, there's no reason to panic

American Elk

The Perfect Shot: Mini Edition for North America

or blunder into the thick vegetation after them. There's a very good chance that they'll come back into the same meadow just before dark.

Elk are extremely hardy creatures that can pack a bad hit for miles. It's usually better to accept a bit of risk in trying to get closer than to attempt a long shot. With an adequate cartridge and a steady position, I don't consider 350 to 400 yards a long shot on elk. You simply must hit them well, because they will often travel fast, far, and hard when poorly hit, and in the rough country where they live you may never catch up.

Taking the Shot

There are no secrets and no mysteries to shot placement. The brain shot is very difficult, with high risk of wounding if you hit low and a risk of wounding and ruining the trophy if you hit high. Lower down in the thick neck it is extremely difficult to visualize exactly where the spine lies. On a neck shot, make it in the upper third of the neck. The target area is not large, but if you place your shot right in the center, you will get your elk.

To my thinking there are really just two sensible options, the lung shot and the shoulder/heart shot, and both are extremely effective. At closer ranges I tend to go for the shoulder/heart shot. It isn't difficult to visualize. Just divide the body into horizontal thirds. With a broadside presentation, come up the centerline of the foreleg into the center of the bottom third. On longer shots I tend to use the lung shot because it offers considerably greater margin for error in all directions—except that, on an animal as big and strong as an

46

American Elk

Now you need a .300 magnum or more, plus a well-constructed bullet.

elk, you must be very careful not to shoot too far back. For the lung shot, again divide the body into horizontal thirds. Come up the rear line of the foreleg into the bottom half of the center third. This shot will take down an elk very quickly.

On angling shots you must visualize where the heart and lungs lie and adjust your hold accordingly. But you must also remember that an elk is not a deer; it is at least two or three times larger and much tougher. You can make angling shots, but only if you have enough gun and enough bullet to absolutely ensure penetration.

The Right Elk

The classic configuration of a mature bull elk is six fighting tines per side. Once in a while a seven-by-seven Rocky Mountain elk is encountered, and the best Roosevelt and tule elk are far more likely to have more than six points. In record-book terms a six-point bull isn't necessarily a big elk. In Boone and Crockett's scoring system, the inside spread, beam length, point length, and four circumferences on each antler are measured.

The elk you can get is dictated largely by what is available in the area you're hunting. Remember, too, that the number of points is just one dimension. A five-by-five is usually a younger bull on its second or third set of antlers, but there are a couple of truly monstrous five-point elk in the record books. Given a choice, I'd take a big five-point over a small six-point.

In an open meadow it's fairly easy to count points and judge the size of a rack, but in the timber it isn't so easy. If you have time, look for a long brow point just over the nose, and

American Elk

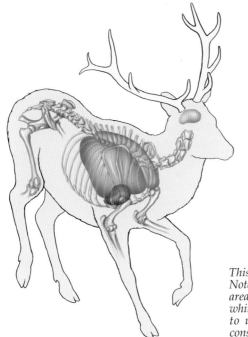

This illustrates an angled shot at an elk. Note how much bone covers the heart/lung area. These are not the bones of a small whitetail. Elk are tough, so it is necessary to use an adequate caliber with well-constructed bullets.

American Elk

American Elk

You do not need to break any major bones to reach the heart or lungs with this shot. However, the margin or error is very small.

The Perfect Shot: Mini Edition for North America

also take a quick look at the fourth point. Called the "dagger" or "sword" point, the fourth point is usually the longest point on a normal elk. If there isn't much time, ignore the bottom of the rack and look for the tip of the main beam. If it forks into a Y with the rearmost point—the actual tip of the main beam—and seems to slant down toward the rump, you are almost certainly looking at a six-point bull. If the main beam tip is straight, you're probably looking at a five-point.

Guns and Loads

There is much controversy surrounding what constitutes the ideal elk rifle. One school of thought is that the standard western deer rifle, typically a .270 Winchester but perhaps as light as a .243 or as heavy as a 7mm Remington Magnum, is perfectly adequate for elk. The other school suggests that you need more gun, a .30-caliber with heavy bullets or, better, something on the order of a fast .33-caliber.

With proper shot placement both are correct. A .270 Winchester will cleanly take any elk that walks. Absent proper shot placement, a .375 H&H will result in a wounded and possibly lost elk, just as if you had used a .243 and had shot in the same place. You have to hit elk well or you're going to have trouble, no matter what you're shooting. Even so, I lean toward the school of larger calibers because a bull elk is a very large and tough animal.

Remember, not all elk are the same. A cow elk usually weighs around 400 to 500 pounds; spike bulls weigh about the same. A "raghorn" bull might weigh a bit more, but it still isn't the same animal as a fully mature bull elk. Though 700 pounds is a good average for a grownup bull, I have seen many tip the scales at more than 800 pounds. You can absolutely kill it with a .270 if everything goes right, but I like the insurance of heavier calibers.

It is extremely difficult to get a shot at such a bull, and you cannot expect more than a couple of chances. If you get any reasonable opportunity to take a good bull, you want to be able to take the shot. You want to be able to take a bull that is standing broadside, quartering strongly away, or quartering to you, and you want to be able to take it at any range from very close to the maximum range at which you are confident you can place your shot.

To my mind, the good old .30-06 with 180-grain bullets is a fine elk cartridge, and in my experience it is far more effective than the .270s and 7mms on large game. However, I believe the best elk cartridges start with the .300 magnums and work upward. My personal favorite is the unpopular and underrated 8mm Remington Magnum, but America's classic elk cartridge is the .338 Winchester Magnum. The faster .33s—the .340 Weatherby Magnum and the .338 Remington Ultra Mag—are not necessarily more effective, but they do extend the range envelope, provided you have the skill to use them. I have actually taken quite a few elk with the .375 H&H, an old-timer that shoots surprisingly flat with some of the lighter bullets available today. It works well—but you don't need an elephant gun to hunt elk. I think you do need plenty of power, but shot placement is what really matters on these big, tough deer.

With a shot like this, the adage "aim for the far shoulder" is apt.

American Elk

Almost straight on and from above is a tough shot. If you can, wait until the bull turns.

Bullet Performance

When you get to animals that are as big and tough as elk, bullet selection is even more important than choice of caliber. Put another way, I'd much rather hunt elk with a .270 Winchester loaded with a good, tough bullet than with a heavier caliber loaded with a quick-expanding "deer bullet." On all game you simply must have enough penetration so that the bullet can reach the vitals, but the larger the game, the more important penetration becomes and the more difficult it is to achieve. Velocity is critical because the more velocity you have, the tougher the bullet must be. Bullet weight mitigates this. A long, heavy-for-caliber 200-grain, .30-caliber bullet doesn't need to be as tough as a 150-grain, .30-caliber bullet in order to ensure penetration, because you have 25 percent more bullet. The lighter the cartridge you are using, the more careful you must be in bullet selection.

Most companies offer a selection, and you need to read the fine print to understand what they're trying to tell you. Nosler's Ballistic Tip bullet is a wonderfully accurate and extremely popular bullet. Read the literature, and you'll see that it's described as an ideal deer bullet. That it is, and stating the positive is the correct marketing approach. What isn't stated but should be inferred is that this is not a good elk bullet! That's what Nosler's good old Partition bullet is for. Winchester has its Ballistic Silvertip, a great deer bullet, but its Fail Safe is a great elk bullet. Federal's Trophy Bonded Bear Claw is a great elk bullet. The Barnes X-Bullet is a great elk bullet. The Swift A-Frame is a great elk bullet, although Swift's new Scirocco is probably tough enough. On elk bullets selection matters, so choose wisely!

It looks like the bull has spotted the hunter.
If he turns, you will likely have no shot.
Shoot now and go for the heart/lung shot.

American Elk

With a slightly going-away angle, the shoulder shot becomes impractical. The heart and lung shots are marked.

Moose

MOOSE
A giant of a deer . . .

In order to really appreciate a moose, the world's largest deer, you need to see it up close. Its bulbous nose and dangling dewlap give it a comical appearance—but at its largest it stands taller than a horse, weighs as much as a Cape buffalo, and carries the biggest and heaviest headgear of any animal on earth. The best time to appreciate this animal is when it's standing on the edge of the bogs and willow thickets that moose love. The worst place is just after you've walked up on your first moose and you suddenly realize you don't have a clue how you're going to get it back to camp.

The moose is North America's second-largest game animal after the bison and the largest game animal that is commonly hunted. It is generally a creature of wilderness, northern forests, and willow-lined lakes and streams. It is rarely hunted where there are roads, and in much of its typically boggy habitat hunters can use horses.

The moose is a grand game animal. Its palmated antlers can spread to spectacular dimensions. During the rut it is known to charge freight trains. That's not a contest it can win, but when it's love-crazed it might charge you—and that's a battle it can win! As big as the moose is, its forests and mountains are bigger. A moose can be almost impossible to find when it doesn't want to be found. And yet, when it's feeding on a hillside in the sunlight, you can see the shine of its black hide and the glint of its horns five or six miles away.

61

Moose

The Perfect Shot: Mini Edition for North America

All of our moose, at maturity, grow palmated antlers with widely varying numbers of points coming off the edges of the palm. The best moose have smaller palms (the "brow palm") at the bottom of the rack, with long points jutting forward. Record-book measurements are attained by a mixture of palm height and width, points, and circumference. The most commonly used measurement—outside spread of the total rack—is the measurement best understood, but it may not be the most important. With Shiras moose, antlers with a spread of 40 inches should be considered very good. In the east a 50-inch moose is superb, but in northern British Columbia you can seek 60-inchers. The latter figure is a darned good moose anywhere, but spreads of 70 inches or more are quite possible with Alaska-Yukon moose.

Shots at Moose

As is the case with so many North American animals, the shot you get at a moose depends not only on where you're hunting but also on your hunting techniques. In mountainous or hilly country, whether in Newfoundland, Alaska, or Colorado, most moose are taken by spot-and-stalk hunting. Moose are huge creatures that can be seen at vast distances, provided they step out of the heavy cover. As with any stalking situation, once you start you never know exactly what's going to happen. The animal might be gone by the time you get there, you might stalk in very close, or you might get hung up by obstacles and need to take a longer shot.

Notice how far forward at an angle the heart lies when the animal is pointing away from the hunter. On the other hand, it is easy to shoot at this angle in front of the heart, so a lung shot is preferable here since the lungs offer a much larger target.

Moose

Moose

Even at this angle, a moose has plenty of vitals exposed—heart, shoulder, and lungs.

Moose

The Perfect Shot: Mini Edition for North America

I'm not convinced that moose see as well as most other antlered animals, but that huge nose is sensitive, and so are those monstrous ears. If you're careful with the noise and keep the wind in your favor, you can often get fairly close to moose.

Longer shots may be necessary almost anywhere, but, in much of the country where moose are hunted, extremely close shots are actually the norm. In the heavy forests of Maine and eastern Canada, shots tend to be very close, and, anywhere moose are hunted, calling is a primary tactic during the rut. Like most animals, moose get extremely silly during the rut. Imitating a moose's low, resonant bellow is an extremely effective way to lure moose out of thick vegetation. Like all other types of calling, it will not work all the time, nor on all moose, but it does work. When a bull moose comes to call, the game changes just a bit. As always, the shooting distance depends on terrain and vegetation, but a love-sick bull moose comes in charged with adrenaline and full of aggression. Under certain circumstances moose can be extremely dangerous. It would be unwise to ignore this fact.

Taking the Shot

The moose is a huge animal, but I have never thought of it as particularly tough. Moose seem to have a slow nervous system that doesn't respond well to bullet shock, but they don't seem to travel very far after receiving a good hit. I've seen moose show absolutely no reaction to well-placed hits with powerful rifles. Instead of heading to the far horizon,

Moose

however, they have generally walked or trotted a few more yards and then toppled over without additional fanfare. I don't think it's particularly hard to kill a moose, but it's extremely hard to drop one.

It also can be extremely important to drop a moose. You know the adage: "The best place is between the ruts. Wheel ruts, that is." There are very few roads or tracks in moose country, but there are streams, ponds, bogs, lakes, and patches of extremely dense willow. The first rule in moose hunting is never to shoot a moose when it's in the water. It's better not to shoot it when it's chest-deep in heavy cover, but at least you can clear away the underbrush. If you have moose down in cold water, you have a nightmarish experience ahead of you. The obvious corollary to this is that no matter where your moose is standing, water and heavy cover are almost certainly nearby. In my entire life I have seen very few animals take a bullet and run to a place where recovery was made easier!

If you're a thinking hunter—and moose recovery is such a huge job that you'd better be thinking about it—you will shoot your mooose while it's in an area that won't hinder field-dressing and recovery. And you'll try to keep it there.

At extremely close range a head or neck shot might be a good option. Both are extremely tricky shots, but moose are so large that a brain shot is unlikely to ruin the trophy. Either shot will certainly drop a moose in its tracks. Just remember that these are difficult shots; the brain is small, lying somewhere between the ears, and there is a great risk of hitting nothing but nasal passages, of which the moose has plenty. The neck

67

Moose

Moose

Heart and low and higher lung shots indicated.

Moose

The Perfect Shot: Mini Edition for North America

shot is easier to visualize; there's a lot of neck, but the spine stays pretty much in the middle for roughly the upper half of the neck. After that it gets trickier, with the spine dropping down and coming into the body cavity a bit lower than you might think.

When I had a Shiras moose tag in Wyoming in 2000, I crawled up within about sixty yards of a bedded bull. All I could see was the head and part of the neck, and I have such an ingrained distrust of the neck shot that I didn't really want to take the shot. I thought about it. The obvious alternative was to wait for the bull to stand, but we were in tight quarters, and I thought if the wind shifted slightly it might leap out of its bed and head for the nearby timber. I would have a shot, but it might be a going-away shot at a running moose. These are things you always have to weigh. I weighed them and took the neck shot, hitting the bull centrally in the neck about a foot behind the ear. It never got up.

The biggest target zone by far is the lung area, not much smaller than the average Dutch door. This is also the easiest shot to visualize. On a broadside presentation, just go up the rear line of the foreleg and shoot your moose right in the middle. It might be a bit better to shoot it slightly below the middle, but either way you have a dead moose. The problem is that this shot will not seem to impress your moose very much. Come to think of it, I've shot moose three or four times in the lungs with very powerful rifles before anything seemed to happen. All shots after the first were unnecessary—but how do you know?

Moose

70

Other than using brain or spine shots, which are tricky, it is very difficult to anchor a moose. The shoulder/heart shot, although it damages more good meat than a lung shot, will do a better job of dropping a moose quickly. Use the centerline of the foreleg, and come up into the bottom third of the body. That shot will break the shoulder and penetrate the heart or the major vessels leading to the heart—if you have enough gun and enough bullet. If you have a bit more, the bullet will keep going and will damage the opposite shoulder as well.

The Right Moose

Really good moose are scarce these days. There are more wolves than ever before. There is also more resident hunting pressure in many parts of both Alaska and Canada. Resident hunters think of the moose as an extremely important meat source, so the "right moose" is a legal animal that will provide tender meat and won't be too much of a nightmare to recover. Some nonresident hunters are also in search of good venison, God bless 'em, but most are looking for antlers.

Relying too heavily on spread alone can be dangerous. With Shiras moose and eastern moose, a "40-inch bull" is probably pretty good. In western Canada a bull from 50 to 55 inches is almost certainly shootable, and with Alaska-Yukon moose you need to look very hard at any bull from 55 inches upward. Just remember that, as is the case with all other antlered game, spread is just one criterion. Look at the presence or

Moose

absence of brow palms, the width of the upper palms or "paddles," and the number of points. Then make your decision based on the appearance of the entire rack, not just some preset spread criterion that you feel you must achieve.

Guns and Loads

Moose are not hard to kill, but they're incredibly hard to put down quickly, and within broad limits I'm not sure really big guns make a difference. I've seen moose taken cleanly, but not quickly, with .270s and .280s. I've personally taken moose very cleanly but no more quickly with .375s and .416s. This is probably the range of cartridges that will work. To my thinking the sheer size of the animal suggests that our common deer cartridges from .270- to .30-caliber are on the light side. Although a moose can weigh as much as a Cape buffalo, I'm also quite certain that you don't need dangerous-game cartridges like .375s and .416s. They certainly work, but the moose is so casual about bullet shock that the big guns won't impress it as much as you think.

My own best results have come with medium-bores. The proper choice depends on whether you expect to take a longer shot. I have used the little .358 Winchester with excellent results, and I absolutely upended a very big Alaskan bull with a .35 Whelen in one of the most spectacular one-shot kills of my entire career. In more open country, faster, flatter-shooting cartridges like the 8mm Remington Magnum and the fast .33s are probably better choices. Mind you, moose are moose, and the immediate results of your perfect shot may not be

Moose

72

spectacular. That relatively small Shiras moose I shot on the aspen ridge in British Columbia was typical. I was sure of the hold, and I shot it three times. Each time I could hear the bullet hit, but I never saw a reaction to the shot, and the bull simply walked off the ridge. That's where we found it, stone dead with the three bullet holes grouped within about six inches on its shoulder. No matter what you are shooting, this is not unusual with moose.

Bullet Performance

Choice of bullet is actually much more important than choice of cartridge. You simply must get the bullet into the vitals, and this means you have a lot of moose to penetrate to get there. I like heavy-for-caliber bullets, and I almost always use 220-grain bullets in my 8mm and 250-grain bullets in my .33s and .35s. With heavy-for-caliber bullets like these, the construction of the bullet isn't quite as critical. My 8mm likes Sierra bullets, and with 220 grains to play with they are tough enough. My .358 likes 250-grain Speers, and with that weight and the cartridge's mild velocity the Speer is plenty tough enough. But in general you should choose bullets no less tough than a Nosler Partition. If you are hunting moose with lighter calibers, then choice of bullet becomes even more important. If you're using cartridges from .270- to .30-caliber, it's especially important to think about heavy-for-caliber, controlled-expansion bullets like the Nosler Partition, Swift A-Frame, Barnes X-Bullet, and Winchester Fail Safe. No matter what you're shooting, you must have penetration, and ultimately it is the bullet, never the cartridge, that will give it to you.

Moose

The angle for a shot is perfect, and a heart or lung shot is ideal in this case as either would minimize meat damage.

CARIBOU
Take him when you see him!

Caribou hunting is a bit different from hunting most other North American big game. Our caribou, *Rangifer tarandus,* are primarily creatures of the northern tundra. They exist, primarily in regional herds, from the northern edges of the forests all the way up to barren islands well north of the Arctic Circle. Come to think of it, their range extends to Greenland, then across northern Europe all the way to Siberia, because our caribou and the reindeer of northern Europe and Asia are slightly different varieties of the same species. All told, there are millions of caribou.

With this many caribou it might seem that this is an easy animal to hunt. Indeed, caribou hunting can be an extremely simple matter—if the caribou happen to be where you are looking for them. Even though the animals are numerous, the northern lands where they live are incredibly vast. Caribou are strongly migratory, constantly moving from summer range to winter range and back again in an endless cycle as they literally vacuum the lichen from the tundra. Although we know the general migration routes of the major herds, it's an imperfect cycle.

Either cold weather or warm weather can accelerate or retard migration. Human activity, such as mineral or energy development, can cause major shifts in the migration route. A classic example is the Trans-Alaska Pipeline, which cut across the traditional

Caribou

A picture-perfect shot. Any decent bullet from a medium-sized caliber will do for a caribou bull in this position. A shot at the top of the heart will do minimum meat damage and ensure a quick death.

migration route of Alaska's Porcupine herd. Also, the migration route naturally shifts over time, as do herd dynamics. The lichen that provides the caribou's primary food is, like almost all Arctic perennials, an extremely slow-growing plant, requiring as long as twenty-five years to mature. The tundra is vast—but so is a herd of several hundred thousand caribou. As the lichen is depleted along a given "axis of advance," to use the military term, the migration route shifts. Sometimes, over a surprisingly short period, the herd numbers plummet, as smaller groupings break off and establish fresh herds in new country.

This boom-and-bust cycle is the natural order of things for many species, but with modern management, agriculture, and developed water sources, we have stopped or at least altered the cycle of many southern species. Caribou still live in wild country that is largely unaltered by the hand of man, so in many northern regions their cycle continues unbroken. For instance, Quebec's well-known George River herd has decreased dramatically during the past decade, and it is believed that the burgeoning Leaf River herd to the west is essentially an offshoot. The new world-record Alaska-Yukon barren ground caribou, taken recently by West Virginian Dan Dobbs, came not from the Mulchatna herd but from a smaller, breakaway group a bit farther south.

The good news is that, except for extremely unusual weather conditions, caribou patterns and dynamics change relatively slowly, and those patterns are known. Also, the caribou migration isn't a single mad rush but a slow and steady advance across a broad front. When the migration is at its peak, a major herd may take several weeks to pass

The Perfect Shot: Mini Edition for North America

through, and there will be a slower trickle of caribou in the lead, in the rear, and on the flanks. So, with proper planning, there should be at least some caribou, even if you don't quite catch the migration. If you really miss it, whether due to poor planning, a sudden shift, or unusual weather conditions, there isn't much you can do about it except enjoy the scenery and maybe get in some good fishing!

This is not about gloom and doom. Caribou hunting is extremely successful—on average, more successful than almost any other North American hunting—because of the number of animals, the fact that caribou are extremely visible in their wide-open country, and the general knowledge of their movement patterns. Just being in good country and hunting hard may not be enough, however. If there are caribou around, you will probably be successful, but if they just aren't present, there isn't much you can do about it!

The caribou generally weighs as much as a midsize deer. A bull's body weight ranges from 275 pounds—about the size of an average mature mule deer—up to as much as 600 pounds (though this is rare) in areas where feed is exceptionally good. For record-keeping purposes we have divided our caribou into regional groupings, loosely based on average antler size. Biologically, the woodland caribou extends along the forest fringes from Newfoundland all the way to British Columbia and southern Yukon. All the record-keeping organizations have subdivided this caribou into three categories: the woodland caribou of Newfoundland and south-central Canada; the larger-antlered Quebec-Labrador caribou of northern Quebec and Labrador; and the mountain caribou of northern British Columbia, southern Yukon, and the Mackenzie district of Northwest Territories.

The Alaska-Yukon barren ground caribou of Northwest Territories' barrens are actually a unique, slightly smaller subspecies (*Rangifer tarandus groenlandicus*), and they are separated as central Canada barren ground caribou. To the west, the largest-antlered caribou of Alaska and northern Yukon are also a distinct subspecies, *Rangifer tarandus granti*, what we hunters call "barren ground caribou." To the north, on the Arctic Islands, there are a few small herds of the pure, very pale Peary caribou, but most Arctic Islands herds are a genetic mixture of Peary caribou and caribou from the mainland. Recognizing this, Safari Club International now recognizes these small-bodied, small-antlered caribou as Arctic Islands caribou.

Shots at Caribou

The hunting of all of these caribou is actually very similar. This business of hunting "resident caribou" is generally a misnomer. All caribou migrate from summer to winter range; it's just a matter of degree. The northern herds may migrate hundreds of miles, while mountain and woodland caribou may migrate just a few miles, from summer range in high valleys and plateaus to winter range in lower country. Given that caribou country is almost always roadless and is usually some combination of boggy, soggy, steep, and rough, if the caribou you wish to hunt are "hung up" just ten miles away, in many cases it

At this angle, all three vital points are exposed.

The Perfect Shot: Mini Edition for North America

may as well be a thousand miles! So you have to hunt caribou where they are, in the hope that your location and their location coincide.

It's a glassing hunt, requiring good optics and generally fast decisions. When you see the right caribou, you must move on it, make sure of it, and then take the shot as quickly as you are able. Caribou are usually on the move, and they move much better in their country than you possibly can.

This is not universal. A bull or group of bulls may hang up in a certain area for a day or two, or they may pass through an area, then reverse and come right back through if the wind changes. Like most ungulates, they often bed through the warmer part of the day, and if you find a bedded bull, you may have several hours to stalk it. But most caribou that you glass will be moving, and if they're really on the move a human cannot stay with them. So you hunt caribou from the front, not from the rear. You must make your decision before caribou pass your location, and if you see one that looks good, you'd better hustle.

Despite the extremely open country, it usually isn't that difficult to get within reasonable shooting range of caribou. Caribou are not particularly wary of man, so an approach within 200 yards is generally practical. Long shooting is possible but rarely essential. Exceptions might include really great bulls that have already passed you or that you can't approach directly because there are obstacles in the terrain or other caribou are in the way. I have hunted caribou in Newfoundland, Quebec, Northwest Territories, Yukon, British Columbia, and Alaska. I don't recall ever shooting at a caribou at genuinely long range, and I'm not even sure I've shot at one past 300 yards. I have taken most of my caribou between one hundred and 200 yards.

Taking the Shot

The average caribou is not much larger than the average deer. Woodland caribou and mountain caribou tend to be bigger and blockier in the body, and there are a few special cases such as the caribou introduced on Adak Island in the Aleutian chain. In the absence of predators and parasites, these caribou are giants, sometimes weighing more than 700 pounds.

Regardless of size, the caribou is not a particularly hardy animal. Hit reasonably well, a caribou will generally not travel very far. However, this animal doesn't respond well to "bullet shock." I have seen many caribou exhibit absolutely no reaction to a well-placed and obviously fatal shot. For this reason one-shot kills are relatively uncommon.

American hunters have a bad habit of concentrating on placing that first shot, then waiting for it to take effect. An African professional hunter I know calls this "admiring the shot." On dangerous game it can be a fatal error, but on any game it's a bad idea because you're banking heavily on your first shot going where you think it did, and on your bullet performing as you think it should. I believe strongly in backing up the first shot if it doesn't immediately take effect. A well-hit caribou will not travel very far, but a poorly hit caribou can travel far and fast. You can't keep up with it, and the chances are slim that it will move into an area where you can recover it more easily or pack it a lesser distance.

This is a tricky shot; shoot too far to the left, and a non-fatal wound might occur. Careful: Do not aim too high, either!

The Perfect Shot: Mini Edition for North America

I believe in hitting a caribou very hard, and if the effects aren't immediate, hit it again until it goes down. Because of its resistance to bullet shock and because the recovery of caribou is generally a matter of packing the meat by hand, I also much prefer a shoulder shot that will break heavy bone and anchor the animal as quickly as possible. The target isn't as large as it is on the behind-the-shoulder lung shot, but it's plenty large enough. On a broadside presentation, just follow the centerline of the foreleg one-third of the way up the body.

The Right Caribou

Caribou grow the largest antlers in relation to body size of any antlered game in the world. Unlike most deer, females also grow small, rudimentary racks. The problem for most beginning caribou hunters is that all caribou look big. This is especially true for hunters accustomed to much smaller-antlered game such as whitetails. It takes a bit of knowledge and extremely good optics to sort them out because caribou also have the most complex racks of any antlered game.

Most of us start by judging the overall size of the rack. In profile, the total rack should appear almost as tall as the animal is from ground to shoulder. Width varies a lot, but the rack should also appear well outside the body from both front and rear. After you've got such a caribou, you look at the various features. Most caribou have a big brow tine that we call a shovel. Optimally, the shovel should reach toward the end of the nose and should be fairly broad. Everybody wants a "double shovel," but two brow tines are fairly

Caribou

uncommon in many areas. A double shovel really isn't that important, and in most cases the second shovel, if present, will be weaker than the first. If you're serious about a record-book bull, however, note that it's very difficult to get a single-shovel bull into Boone and Crockett, regardless of the caribou's other attributes.

Then move up to the bez, a secondary point or palmated cluster of points about a quarter of the way up from the shovel. You want the bez to be long and, hopefully, multi-pointed, something like an outstretched hand. About halfway up the main beam, facing rearward, there may be back points. These are not present in all caribou, even in really good ones, so they are almost like bonus points. Really good, matching back points add a lot to the record-book score. Now take a look at the top points. These are important to the impressive appearance of a rack. Note, however, that most scoring systems (Boone and Crockett and Pope and Young) only measure the length of the two longest top points.

Beam length, mass, and inside spread are also important. There's a lot to look at on a caribou, and if the animals are moving, you must look quickly and make up your mind. It isn't easy, and it takes practice. No caribou, even the very best heads, "have it all" in equal proportion, so you must make trade-offs while you're looking. There's also a question of preference. I like top points, while others prefer double shovels. No two racks are alike, which is part of the fun in hunting any antlered game.

There are numerous record-book categories for caribou, but the differences among them are not that great. Woodland caribou have the smallest, most compact rack, usually with many

The Perfect Shot: Mini Edition for North America

points, but the tops tend to be weak and the beams are relatively short. Quebec-Labrador caribou are known for strong bez formations, and mountain caribou, at their best, have spectacular top points. Alaskan caribou are known for long beams that, typically, form a big C. If you took a record-class caribou from each category and put them on the wall side by side, very few people could correctly identify each of them. So pay attention to what constitutes a good caribou for the area you're hunting, and look carefully at each feature of the complex rack. When there are lots of caribou moving, sorting through them to find the bull that pleases you most is the real fun of caribou hunting!

Guns and Loads

Caribou are neither particularly large nor particularly tough. The Inuit hunt them for meat with the rifles they have; the most popular calibers are .222 Remington, .30-30, and .303 British. This suggests that a .243 or .25-caliber would be perfectly adequate. It might be, if everything goes right, but trophy hunting is different from meat hunting. You want to take the best caribou you can find, and when you find it you want to be able to drop it.

Two factors suggest that somewhat more powerful or flatter-shooting cartridges, or both, are appropriate. First, although long shots are usually not necessary, there is certainly the potential for them on the open tundra. Second, wind is almost always a factor. Fast cartridges from about .270 to .30-caliber buck the wind a whole lot better than slower cartridges, or even very fast cartridges of lesser caliber.

Caribou

I think ideal caribou cartridges start with the .270 Winchester or a very fast 6.5mm (like the old .264 Winchester Magnum) and go up through the 7mms to the fast .30s. There is no reason to hunt caribou with a cartridge larger in caliber than .30. But if you're combining caribou with moose, grizzly bear, or brown bear, you might consider a flat-shooting medium-magnum like one of the .33s, from .338 Winchester Magnum up through the .338 Remington Ultra Mag. and the .340 Weatherby Magnum.

Bullet Performance

While the caribou is just a bit on the large side for the really quick-opening bullets, you really don't need the deepest-penetrating designs like Barnes X-Bullet, Swift A-Frame, or Winchester Fail Safe. There is nothing wrong with using them—they are certainly a good idea if you're combining caribou with tougher, larger game, such as bear or moose. But for pure caribou hunting, I like bullets that offer a combination of expansion and penetration. This means that the good old Nosler Partition is extremely hard to beat.

I recently used the new Swift Scirocco bullet, a polymer-tipped bullet that has a lead core chemically bonded to a relatively thick jacket. The polymer tip ensures expansion, while the bonded core and heavy jacket ensure weight retention—and the design has a high ballistic coefficient, ideal for longer shooting in windy country. The Scirocco is useful in a lot of hunting applications, but it's especially ideal for hunting open-country game that is a bit bigger than deer but not especially large or tough.

The heart shot may also break the shoulder bone when the leg is extended back like this. The lower dot indicates the heart shot, while the upper dot indicates the lung shot.

Pronghorn Antelope

PRONGHORN ANTELOPE
The classic open-country game animal . . .

America's pronghorn antelope is a truly magnificent creature, perfectly adapted to the wide-open plains it calls home. It has fabulous eyesight—certainly the best among all North American game—and the eyes are its first line of defense, though not its most important asset. It is built for speed, with outsize lungs, feet cushioned to take the pounding, and seemingly spindly legs that have the tensile strength of a cow's legs.

The pronghorn is not actually an antelope, and in fact it has no particularly close relatives anywhere in the world. Its Latin name, *Antilocapra americana*, describes it as the "American antelope-goat," which is a pretty fair description. It looks like an antelope, but it has many characteristics common to the goat family. It also has features that belong to no other animal. Unlike antelope and goat, which have true horns that form around a bony core and continue to grow throughout the animal's life, the pronghorn sheds its headgear annually, leaving a daggerlike core around which the new horns form. These horns aren't of the same material as most horns. They are more like solidified hair, a pure protein material that is probably closer to rhinoceros horn than anything else now living on the planet. The coat is unusual, too. Its relatively thick, stiff, hollow hairs give pronghorn great insulation against the bitter prairie winters.

When the front leg of any animal is fully extended backward as in this picture, it is easy to make the mistake of shooting a little too far back. Mentally keep the whole picture of the chest cavity in mind, and remember that the entire heart and much of the lungs lie in front of the leg bone in this position.

Pronghorn Antelope

Pronghorn Antelope

The pronghorn is a relatively small, dainty animal, with mature bucks rarely weighing much more than 120 pounds and standing about 36 inches at the shoulder. Most authorities identify five regional subspecies: *Antilocapra americana americanca*, the pronghorn found throughout most of the West; *Antilocapra americana oregona*, the pronghorn of southeastern Oregon; *Antilocapra americana mexicana*, from southeastern Arizona eastward to Texas and down into central Mexico; *Antilocapra americana sonoriensis*, west of *mexicana*; and *Antilocapra americana peninsularis*, originally from Southern California down into the Baja Peninsula. The latter two are considered endangered, but the differences between the subspecies are very subtle, and biologists have never fully agreed on where one subspecies stops and another starts. No record-keeping organization has ever attempted to differentiate the pronghorn subspecies.

Pronghorn occur naturally in the plains, valleys, and foothills from the Great Plains west to California, and from northern Mexico to southern Canada. At one time they existed in untold millions, almost certainly more numerous than even the bison, but by the early years of the twentieth century, some naturalists predicted total extinction. Fortunately, this didn't happen. Last-minute protection saved remnant herds, and the prolific pronghorn has made a strong comeback.

The pronghorn needs relatively undisturbed prairie, so it doesn't do particularly well in areas with intensive agriculture. It is once again quite plentiful in ranch country and badlands throughout the West. Today all pronghorn hunting is by limited permit, mostly by

The Perfect Shot: Mini Edition for North America

drawing, but there are lots of opportunities. Wyoming probably has the most habitat and certainly has the largest population, but pronghorn are also plentiful in suitable habitat in Montana, Colorado, and New Mexico. There are also considerable populations, though much more localized, in Arizona, California, Oregon, Nevada, and Utah. Pronghorn are much less plentiful on the eastern and northern edges of their domain—west Texas; the high plains of western Kansas, Nebraska, and the Dakotas; and the prairies of southern Canada—but, depending on current game counts, all of these areas have open seasons and offer some permits.

The areas that produce the very best pronghorn trophies are extremely difficult to draw, which is the case with most animals that are hunted by drawing a permit. Arizona, for instance, is legendary for big pronghorn—and drawing a tag is almost as difficult as drawing a sheep tag. Though you may not always draw the tag you want, pronghorn tags aren't that hard to come by. It's fairly easy to draw a tag in most areas in eastern Wyoming, eastern Montana, and eastern Colorado, and although they are more expensive, private land tags are available in New Mexico and a few other places.

With its buff-and-white body, black nose, and unique horns, the pronghorn is a striking animal—and it also stands out in its wide-open terrain. Despite its legendary eyesight and great speed, it is relatively easy to hunt. One factor is that it is visible at great distances; another is simply that, in most areas where pronghorn are hunted, the animals are quite common.

Pronghorn Antelope

Most outfitted hunts are fairly inexpensive—especially when compared with other western hunts. But it's also quite possible to hunt pronghorn just as successfully unguided. The latter is a practical option. It takes a bit more research to make absolutely certain you have a good place to hunt, but you'll find that you can take unguided hunts in some areas that have plenty of public land. You will also find that a lot of the best pronghorn habitat is tied up in private ranches.

Shots at Pronghorn

There are several misconceptions about pronghorn hunting. One is that it requires long-range shooting. An even bigger misconception is this business about racing across the prairie in a vehicle, trying to get close enough to throw lead at these speedsters. I'll dispense with the latter first. Chasing pronghorn in a vehicle is not only unsporting, unethical, and usually illegal, it's also a terrible way to get a shot. The pronghorn antelope is thought to be the second-fastest creature in the animal kingdom. Only the cheetah is believed to be capable of greater speed—but the cheetah is short-winded, while the pronghorn can sustain speeds of more than forty miles per hour for extended distances. Yes, you can get close to them in a vehicle, provided you don't destroy your rig in the process, but then you are faced with takin a running shot at an animal that's going like hell. Shot placement is impossible, judging horns almost equally so.

It isn't necessary to try to run them down, and it usually isn't necessary to shoot at extreme range. Mind you, at first glance pronghorn country looks like a billiard table, and

Pronghorn Antelope

Aim at the point where the neck joins the body and this buck is yours.

Pronghorn Antelope

The Perfect Shot: Mini Edition for North America

it's only natural for beginning pronghorn hunters to believe they must reach clear across its broad expanse. Sometimes you must, for you will find there are sagebrush flats that offer almost no cover. Because of hunting pressure, moreover, pronghorn tend to know they are safe in such places. But if you study the country carefully, it usually isn't all that flat and featureless. There are usually almost imperceptible little gullies and coulees and folds, and if you read the ground correctly and put in a bit of effort, it is usually possible to get pretty darned close.

Of course, "close" is a relative term. Shots at pronghorn probably do average somewhat longer than shots at most game animals. My average shot at a pronghorn usually does not exceed 200 yards. For hunters accustomed to close shots at whitetail in thick cover, a 200-yard shot at a smaller animal in unfamiliar, wide-open country can seem like a very long poke. Though much current literature suggests that quarter-mile shots are necessary, the 200-yard shot is a whole lot different and much more practical.You can readily see pronghorn way out there at the very edge of practical shooting distance—and if they haven't been disturbed, they probably won't spook. So the first principle is to recognize that you really need to get a bit closer in order to be sure. The second principle lies in recognizing that you usually can get closer and trying to figure out how.

Most of the time the ground isn't quite as flat as it looks. Most of the prairie is cut by shallow drainages and low ridges, and much sagebrush is tall enough to offer some cover. It doesn't take much relief to hide a pronghorn—but it does take some effort to hide you from their sharp eyes. With pronghorn hunting, the whole idea is to use good optics to judge the horns from as far away as possible. Once you find one that looks good enough or is worth a closer look, you need to find a way to drop out of sight—and not reappear until you're within good, sure shooting range, whatever that means to you. You should try to keep the wind in your favor, but this is small change compared to the need to stay out of sight.

Sometimes you can use hills and ridges to make a circle, but most likely you will eventually have to start crawling. This is backbreaking work, and the stuff is prickly. In warm weather you need to keep an eye out for rattlesnakes, and in any weather little prairie cacti will bedevil your hands and knees. Thick leather gloves are a must, and a lot of serious pronghorn hunters use knee and elbow pads. Maybe I have a masochistic streak, but crawling within certain range of a chosen buck is, to me, the real fun of pronghorn hunting! It means beating these sharp-eyed creatures at their own game in their own country, and it's a wonderfully satisfying experience.

Sometimes you can get very close. Dwight van Brunt (then of Burris) and I were hunting on the Gros Ventres Indian Reservation in Montana a few years ago, a place where, at that time, two pronghorns were allowed. For my second buck I borrowed Dwight's XP-100 pistol, chambered to 7mm-08 Remington. I shoot the specialty pistols a bit, and I knew a long shot was out, but I figured I was OK out to 200 yards or so. We glassed a nice buck working its way from an open flat toward a system of ridges, so we got ourselves in front of the buck,

99

The Perfect Shot: Mini Edition for North America

thinking it would walk through a little saddle maybe 150 yards away. The pronghorn thought differently. We hadn't seen it for quite a while, and then it materialized out of a little cut less than forty yards away, heading straight toward us. I shot it from about 25 yards, little more than a blur of white and tan through the pistol scope's narrow field.

Not all stalks work. Sometimes you wind up spooking the animal, or you can easily misread the situation and run out of cover before you get as close as you need to get. That doesn't necessarily mean the game is over, although it might be over for that particular day. Pronghorn country looks much the same to you and to me, but it doesn't look the same to the animals. They are surprisingly territorial, which offers two opportunities. Unless spooked quite badly, a pronghorn buck will usually be reluctant to leave its home ground. It probably won't run that far, which means that you can let it run out of sight and then follow.

When you've spooked a pronghorn, it isn't always practical or smart to follow it up; this depends on the terrain it's gone into. But that doesn't mean the hunt is over. If you leave the pronghorn alone, there is a very good chance it will come right back to the place where you first saw it—if not later the same day, then almost certainly by the next day. This doesn't necessarily mean exactly the same place, but it does mean the same general area. That's why scouting for pronghorn a day or two before the season is so effective, especially in areas that have very short seasons and/or a lot of hunting pressure. Pronghorn are as habitual as they are territorial. Unless they are seriously disturbed, usually you will find them not only in the same general areas, but also doing the same things in the same places at the same time of day. If you find a good buck watering at one o'clock on the day before opening day, chances are it will be at that watering hole between twelve and two unless another hunter waylays it. Pronghorn also tend to cross fences in exactly the same place. By the way, it is not true that pronghorn can't jump fences. I've seen them do it. It is true they prefer to go under or through a fence, and their crossings are usually well marked with trails and scraped hair.

Sometimes a long shot is the only option you've got. A couple of years ago, hunting with Leica's Terry Moore, gunmaker Lex Webernick, and guide Fred Lamphere, we found a really good pronghorn way out on a sagebrush flat. That darned flat was almost in perfect position. On the west side was a range of low hills that offered perfect cover right to the edge. On the east side was a winding, cottonwood-lined streambed, so getting to that side of the flat was a simple matter of a pleasant stroll along the cottonwoods. The problem was that the flat was about 1,200 yards wide, and the buck and its herd tended to stay right in the middle, too long a shot from either side.

Fred and I strolled to the cottonwoods, crossed the creek, and then crawled out to the fence line without spooking the herd. At this point "close" became a relative matter: Through my Leica rangefinder, the buck was 454 yards away. I was using an extremely accurate .300 Weatherby Magnum that day, so I had plenty of gun, and I knew the range and the hold. I got the buck—but that's the longest shot I've attempted on a pronghorn in at least thirty-five years!

Pronghorn Antelope

Here you need to lead a bit to hit the heart/lung area.

The Perfect Shot: Mini Edition for North America

Taking the Shot

The pronghorn is not a large animal. In fact, when you walk up on your first buck, you'll probably be surprised at its actual size. That's because its thick hair combined with its bright color makes it look much bigger than it really is. They are, however, extremely tough for their size, and if they're hit poorly—taking a leg wound or a paunch shot, for example—they seem to be inclined to just keep going for as long as they are able.

This doesn't suggest that you need lots of power. That isn't the issue at all. On an animal the size of a pronghorn, I doubt if there's much difference between a bad hit with a .243 and a bad hit with a .300 magnum. The point is that a bad hit on a pronghorn can result in an extremely long day and, very likely, a lost animal.

The skin of a pronghorn is paper thin and extremely fragile. Also, you have the problem associated with all light-colored animals—the cape is easily stained and hard to fix. So, if you're thinking of saving a buck to have it mounted, a head or neck shot is out of the question.

Many disagree, but to me pronghorn is among the very best wild meat, provided you take proper care of it. This means skinning and cooling it as quickly as possible, and boning the meat to get it away from the strong marrow. If you handle it promptly and well, it's wonderful stuff.

For all these reasons I prefer lung shots on pronghorn. The pronghorn has outsize lungs, so the target area (or, rather, the margin for error) is proportionately larger than on most animals. The shot is absolutely deadly, and, at least from a broadside angle, it damages the skin behind the part needed for a shoulder mount. Finally, the lung shot damages very little edible meat. Placement is standard: On a broadside presentation, follow the back line of the rear leg up into the body, and shoot just a bit below the horizontal midpoint.

The Right Buck

Pronghorn aren't particularly easy to judge. Their jet-black horns tend to look bigger than they really are, especially when the animal is running and most of all from a going-away angle. The best way to view pronghorn is from a distance with good optics, so you can evaluate them dispassionately and unhurriedly. Pronghorn enter the record books based on a combination of horn length (on the outer curve), prong length (from the back of the horn to tip of prong), and circumference (four circumferences—at the base and at the three-quarters). A long prong is fairly obvious, as are exceptionally long horns, but circumference is very hard to judge unless it's really dramatic—as is the case with all game.

The ears are about 6 inches long, and a normal pronghorn buck will have horns about 12 inches long, or double the length of the ears. The hard part is that much of the actual length measurement comes from the downward hook at the tip of the horns, not from the height. So any pronghorn that appears to rise up double the ears (or more) is worth a second look—but if it doesn't have tips that hook around and back down, it's probably not as long as you think it is. People talk about 16- and 17-inch pronghorn, and they exist, but I have never shot one. Since I've never put a tape on one, I can't say for sure I've ever seen one. In most areas a genuine 14-inch pronghorn is pretty darned good, and a 15-inch

The Perfect Shot: Mini Edition for North America

pronghorn is exceptional. Then the other factors come into play: A 15-inch pronghorn with good mass and long prongs will make Boone and Crockett; a spindly 17-incher with short prongs may not.

Keep in mind that pronghorn populations are extremely subject to the vagaries of winter, and, since they grow new horns each year, springtime weather also matters. Not all areas are capable of producing really big pronghorn, even under the best of conditions. The best areas will be better in some years and not so good in others. The best course is to look around and consider what kind of bucks you're seeing. In my experience there will usually be lots of bucks of average size—sometimes 12 inches, sometimes 13 inches, rarely 14 inches. Whatever that "house number" happens to be, there will usually be a few bucks a bit bigger than the average, and those are the ones you're looking for.

Guns and Loads

The primary consideration in a pronghorn rifle is accuracy. Your rifle should be well scoped, it should group well, and you should have absolute confidence in it. Flat-shooting capability is secondary, but you do need it. From the standpoint of the size of the animal, a .243 or fast .25 (.25-06, .257 Weatherby Magnum, et cetera) would be ideal, if you aren't especially concerned about trophy dimensions and you have no interest in attempting genuinely long shots. The problem with the smaller calibers is that, regardless of how fast, wind impacts light bullets more than it does heavier bullets. Pronghorn country is always windy! In years gone by I have rated the .25-06 the most perfect pronghorn cartridge. I no longer think it is, because I recently saw two very good riflemen wound pronghorns between 300 and 400 yards, one with a .25-06, the other with a wildcat .257 STW—and then have trouble finishing the job because the wind was blowing the bullets too much.

Based on these experiences, I think the very best pronghorn cartridges—for all ranges and all conditions—are the fast 6.5mm, .270, and 7mm cartridges. This includes cartridges ranging from the almost-obsolete .264 Winchester Magnum through the .270 Winchester, new .270 Winchester Short Magnum, and .270 Weatherby Magnum, and on up to the many magnum 7mms, including the red-hot 7mm Remington Ultra Mag. Obviously, the .30-calibers will work, and no lesser-caliber bucks the wind better than an aerodynamic .30-caliber. But I can't bring myself to say that you really need a .30-caliber for a 120-pound pronghorn, so I won't!

Bullet Performance

Pronghorn are small and fairly fragile animals, provided you hit them in the right place. I prefer bullets that will open up fairly quickly, but let's not overdo it. Extremely frangible bullets can really make a mess of a pronghorn, and that is absolutely unnecessary. The point is to hit your pronghorn in the right place, and if you do that with any big-game weight bullet from 6mm on up, you should have your pronghorn!

You can judge the inside spread of a deer's rack by comparing it with the distance between the whitetail's ear tips, which is usually 15 to 16 inches.

Field Judging
Deer Racks

FIELD JUDGING DEER RACKS*

by Gerald Almy

The northern Michigan woods glowed saffron in the autumn sunlight and the golden color seemed to radiate from the buck's brown coat as he fed through the meadow. There were other deer out, but this one dwarfed those around him with his body size. The belly sagged and the back swayed down, indicating an older deer.

The rack looked huge, sweeping wide beyond the ears with eight long points jutting upward. The mass stood out in particular, even with the deer's large body.

"He's a good buck," said guide Dan Rosman. "He'll go in the upper 140s, maybe 147."

I wasn't expecting him to pin the score down quite that precisely, but for an eight pointer, those numbers would make an impressive rack.

Tightening my finger on the Ultra Light trigger, I watched as the buck jumped then ran hard, falling just inside the edge of the woods. When we walked up, we found that it was an incredibly large deer with a beautiful tawny coat and eight massive points. Back at the game shed, Dan scored him at 147½ Boone and Crockett points.

I doubt that I'll ever become *that* good at judging an animal's potential score in the field. But over thirty years of deer hunting across North America, often with wildlife biologists and veteran guides who spend not days, but months in the woods and fields each year studying or hunting deer, I've learned some of the tricks they use to estimate with uncanny accuracy the inches of antler on a buck's head.

Field Judging Deer Racks

* Adapted from "Rack 'Em" by Gerald Almy in *Sports Afield,* January 2004.   **109**

The Perfect Shot: Mini Edition for North America

Before going into those field judging techniques, it's worth taking a look at the sometimes controversial issue of scoring deer and other big-game animals. Does it demean or cheapen the hunt and make it a less fulfilling, spiritual experience? I don't think so. Giving a buck's score is a valuable way to describe how large a rack is. It doesn't really say much to call a buck "an eight pointer." An eight pointer could be a precocious yearling with thin horns and a tiny body or a 275-pound six-year-old northern whitetail with 147 inches of antler, like the one I took on the hunt described earlier.

The score of a deer is also important for what it symbolizes. To take a high-scoring buck is to successfully outwit one of the wariest of big-game quarries—an elusive and rare animal that has survived at least three or four hunting seasons, showing special savvy and chariness. He has bred his genes for a number of years, passing them on to future generations, and reached the old age class that is so important to the trophy hunter.

While no one should ever place score as the preeminent concern of a deer hunt, it is a legitimate item to consider, along with the age of the animal. Far from being disrespectful, trophy hunting shows special admiration for the quarry by giving it a chance to live a longer life and reach its prime physical development before trying to harvest it.

Boone and Crockett, Safari Club International, Buckmasters, and Burkett have scoring systems, but B&C is most often used. It's true that the net score in this system penalizes asymmetry and extra kicker points in the typical category, but most hunters simply tally the gross score (before deductions) and use that as the

110

Field Judging
Deer Racks

is deer has outstanding mass and width (an inside spread 21 to 22 inches), and 9- to 11-inch G-2s. It's a brute, but th only eight points, it will score in the low 140s.

This deer packs a lot into a compact rack—it's got at least six points per side and a sticker. But because it has only a 15- to 16-inch inside spread (note the width of the rack compared to the width of the ears), it will probably score a few inches shy of 150.

The Perfect Shot: Mini Edition for North America

important measurement. Net score only comes into play if you want to enter the animal in the record book.

Tactics for Scoring Deer

Most of these comments relate to whitetails, but they are, in large part, applicable to mule deer as well. The first thing to realize about scoring is that you may have lots of time or you may just have seconds before the buck vanishes. I've lost the chance to kill many bucks that in retrospect I should have taken, simply because I wasn't sure at first glance how big they were. On the other hand, we've all rushed decisions and shot bucks we should have let walk.

Before trying to analyze the various antler components and actually compute a score in your head, do an instant ball-park estimate of the score based on your first visual impression. Look at the body or how it compares to other deer in the area first, to make sure you feel it's old enough to harvest (three to five years or older, depending on where you're hunting and the degree of pressure). Next get an image of the rack in your head and a first hunch. Is it a 120-class deer? A 140 or 160? Depending on what type of deer the area holds, this will tell you whether you want to do a more thorough calculation of each component of the rack.

David Morris, author and founding publisher of *North American Whitetail,* says he likes to try to have a "burned in" image of what a 130 buck or a 140 buck or a 150 looks like, then his mind will immediately compare the animal he's looking at in the field with the image stored in his brain. This is an excellent tactic.

Field Judging Deer Racks

Keep in mind, though, that certain things can make that first impression deceiving. For instance, a silhouetted view of antlers always makes them look bigger. Seeing a rack strictly from the back enhances how large it looks, and darker antlers look bigger than pale ones. Also consider the body size of the buck. A deer in the Texas Hill Country may have such a small body that the rack looks bigger than it actually is. A Canadian buck's rack will look small because these animals field dress from 200–300 pounds.

If you're hunting where a 140-inch buck is a tremendous trophy and you think the deer is that good or better and it's about to flee, you may want to just go with your hunch and squeeze the trigger. If possible, though, try the following mental tabulation.

Four measurements are included: inside spread, main beam, and length of tines and mass, taken at four locations on each side. Hunters and guides use different systems to tabulate these scores, but many start with beam length, then add tine length, mass, and finally spread. Whatever order you choose, you need to analyze each trait.

Inside spread is clearly one of the least important factors. This is easy to see since the Jordan buck, the number one typical for nearly eighty years, had only a 20⅛-inch spread. On the other hand, if you want a rack that is impressive and stunning to look at, spread definitely helps. The perfect example is Milo Hanson's 213⅝ world-record buck, which measures 27⅜ inside.

The best way to judge spread is by comparing it with the width between a whitetail's ear tips in its naturally alert position. This will vary from about 14 to 17 inches on a

113

The Perfect Shot: Mini Edition for North America

whitetail, but in most regions it's about 15–16 inches. If a buck's inside spread measures a couple inches outside of each ear, it's definitely above average.

Mass is crucial to a high-scoring buck, and it is also one of the strongest indicators that you're looking at an older deer—at least three years plus. The best deer will not only have good mass at the base and lower points but carry it through most of the main beam. Mass measurements on a whitetail are taken between the antler burr and the brow tine and between the next three sets of points, or halfway between the last point and the end of the beam if the buck is an eight pointer.

One good way to judge mass is by comparing it to a deer's eyeball, which is about 3½–3¾ inches. If it looks bigger than that, it's likely a mature deer. If it's a *lot* bigger, squeeze the trigger. Mass quality is hard for the newcomer to differentiate, but the more deer you look at, the easier it is to tell a medium from a heavy-horned animal.

Main beam length contributes greatly to the score of a buck. Most of the top record-book whitetails have beams over two feet long, up to 30 inches on the Jordan buck and 32 inches on Brian Damery's incredible 200⅝, 17-pointer taken in Illinois in 1993.

This is also a tricky measurement to guess in the field. Bucks whose antlers come mostly straight forward or straight up usually have fairly short beams. The best bucks often have a pronounced curl in the beam that adds length before they sweep forward, and some continue that curl inward before they end. Beams that extend forward to a line drawn vertically with the nose are usually 20 inches or more, but with a lot of curl they could be quite a bit longer than 20.

114

Field Judging Deer Racks

Using a deer's ear as a comparison can help you judge beam length, too. A whitetail's ear is about six to seven inches, so you can extrapolate how many ear lengths the beam seems to be to get a rough idea of its length.

The number of tines is extremely important, since each one is measured (up to seven per side). This is a big handicap for the trophy class eight-point buck. No matter how impressive the main beam, the mass, and the overall beauty of the buck, it's hard to rack up a high score with only the brow tines and two more points on each side measured. (You don't add the last point because it's included in the main beam measurement.) Still, some massive eight pointers will score well, with a few in the record book, including two that netted $180\frac{3}{8}$—one from South Dakota and one from Michigan.

You need a deer to stand still at least momentarily to count points, then a few seconds more to calculate or estimate the length of each point, adding them up in your head as you go. Most bucks are fairly symmetrical, so you don't have to do this twice. You can judge the side you see best and unless the other looks strikingly different, you can figure it's pretty close. On the other hand, if you're strictly interested in a high net score and a typical deer, pay close attention to each side of the rack and compare the points to see where they differ . . . realizing that deductions will be taken out of the final score.

Start with the brow tines or eye guards, considered the first point. Genetics of the local deer herd has a lot to do with the length of this point, but individual deer vary greatly, too.

Instead of going out, this deer goes up. The inside spread is 16½ to 17 inches and the main beam is short. Its brow tines are good, but its other points are only fair. It's a 137 buck.

Good main beams are the strong point of this buck. Its brow tines are 4 to 5 inches long, but with poor second points (G-2s) and an 18- to 19-inch inside spread, this buck will score in the mid-to upper 130s.

Field Judging Deer Racks

A three- to four-inch brow tine is fairly typical on a good buck. The second point should measure at least seven or eight inches on a trophy, and will go ten to twelve inches on high-scoring bucks. The third point is often shorter, but on some bucks it may be longer than the second. Use the length of a deer's ear as a convenient tool to judge the length of points.

The main thing to realize about scoring deer is that the more bucks you look at—alive in the field, on videos, in taxidermy shops and trophy rooms, and at outdoor shows—the more you'll have a "feel" for what a particular deer will score even before you do the tabulations in your head. But by practicing and developing your own system for quickly calculating and adding up the four measurements of inside spread, mass, main beam, and tine length, you'll be able to fine-tune that first "guesstimate" even more precisely. A quality binocular is vital, and a good spotting scope is even better if there's time to use it.

Don't let score become an overwhelming obsession, but look at it as one interesting facet of the whole multidimensional deer hunting experience. And while I'm intrigued with scoring deer, I for one would never pass up a buck I liked and had hunted hard for simply because the score might not compare well with other animals.

Setting Standards

What constitutes a trophy will vary with the location of the hunt. If you hunt in Florida, for instance, you will be setting your sights lower than the hunter who owns a farm in Iowa. You'll be looking for a 120 or 130 buck instead of a 150 or 160.

The Perfect Shot: Mini Edition for North America

Similarly, if you are a young or beginning hunter, the standards for a trophy will be lower. To a 15-year-old who has only harvested does and a spike, a 14-inch wide eight pointer is a great buck, and we should celebrate and encourage that hunter's joy and pride in taking that animal.

Finally, there's simply the matter of personal taste. Some people like high, diamond-shaped racks. They don't score well, but they are attractive. Other people favor a wide spread, insisting that an animal have a 20-inch or more outside measurement. Still others like points the most. I confess my main obsession is mass. Don't try to suppress your personal preferences. Go for a buck that embodies them, but also know what you are giving up in other aspects of the rack and how it will affect the numbers when the final tally is made.

Practicing Technique

Guess the score of mounted bucks in taxidermy shops or at outdoor shows based on your first initial impression. Write that down. Then tabulate in your head methodically what you think the score would be. Now ask the owner what the score of the animal is and see how close you were on both your initial guess and the mentally calculated score. Better still, get the head down off the wall and compare the specific measurements to what you guessed for mass, tine length, main beam, and inside spread. See where you were wrong, then look at the rack again to see how you misjudged it. This is the surest way I know to become an accurate field judge, short of quitting your job and becoming a full-time guide!

Scoring Mule Deer

The same basic measurements are taken on mule deer as whitetails—inside spread, main beam, tine length, and mass. One important difference, however, is that only four points are counted on each side, versus up to seven for a whitetail. This is because the typical mule deer rack has brow tines and then two forks on each side (one point of which is the main beam).

When searching for a good mule deer buck, guides I've hunted with suggest looking for good mass, a spread close to or better than two feet, and, most importantly, deep forks. The deeper the forks, the longer the tines and main beam will be. The G-2s or main back tines should be 14 to 18 inches or more on a trophy buck. On Doug Burris' world record, they measured 22½ inches.

A mule deer's ears are longer than a whitetail's, with eight to nine inches typical. The spread between the ears is wider, too—about 18–21 inches from ear tip to ear tip in the normal alert position, versus 14–17 for a whitetail. If a rack's spread comes out a couple inches on either side of that, and other antler qualities such as mass and tine length look good, it's likely a topnotch buck.

You should look for 20-inch or longer main beams, using the ears again as a handy 8–9 inch "ruler." Finally, consider mass. This can be calculated by comparing the antler's circumference to the eye, which will be around 3½ to 3¾ inches. Most trophy bucks have 4 inches or more of mass between the burr and brow tine.

The Perfect Shot, North America
Shot Placement for North American Big Game
by Craig Boddington

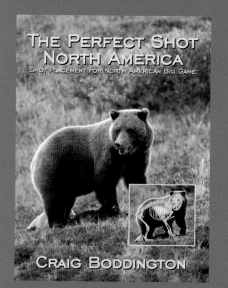

You bought the mini-edition of *The Perfect Shot, North America,* which contains information on whitetail, mule deer, moose, caribou, pronghorn, and elk. Now get the full-size, complete edition that covers all North American big game: the brown bear, grizzly, and black bear, whose vitals must be hit or dangerous situations will ensue; Stone and Dall sheep, as well as the Rocky Mountain and desert bighorns; feral hog and the javelina; polar bear; wolf; goat; muskox; bison; and walrus. Boddington also writes about what guns to use, what calibers he recommends, and what bullet types are suitable for each animal. The larger version also highlights the location of the brain on dangerous game in case a shot is needed to stop a charging animal. Long Beach, 215pp, color and b&w photos, 8.5x11, hardcover with dust jacket.

$39.95, shipping extra.

The Perfect Shot, Africa
by Kevin Robertson

The African edition includes all classes of African game—from the largest, thick-skinned elephant and buffalo, to the large cats, to the antelopes (eland, sable, etc.), and finally to the smallest game animals (duiker and warthog).

$65.00, shipping extra.

Also available:
The Perfect Shot: Mini Edition for Africa
by Kevin Robertson
$17.95, shipping extra.

safaripress.com